My Diane

Barbara Ryder

New Life Publishing
England

Copyright © Barbara Ryder 1999
First published in the UK 1999 by New Life Publishing
Company, PO Box 277, Sunderland, SR1 1YE

All rights reserved. No part of this publication may be
reproduced, stored in a retrieval system, or transmitted in
any form or by any means, electronic, mechanical,
photocopying, recording or otherwise, without the prior
permission of the publisher.

British Library Cataloguing in Publication Data

A catalogue record for this book is available from the
British Library

ISBN 0 9536100 0 4

Printed by Bailes, Houghton le Spring.

Foreword

The vivid detail of events etched out in the pages of this book tell the story of misunderstanding, shattered dreams, heartache and a mother's faith in God that wouldn't take no for an answer. The answer would not be quick in coming; it would take thirty-three years, but faith in God's promises held on. To see and hear Diane now is to witness a marvellous change and there can be no doubt that a wonderful miracle has taken place.

It has been my privilege over the years to be associated with Jack, Barbara and Diane as well as the other members of the family. "My Diane" is their story for their lives have all been so closely interwoven. Through the pages of this book you will enter their lives and in so doing you will feel the hurt and heartache that they have experienced. You will also gain a fresh insight into what it is like to be the parents of a disabled child. Through it all an unshakeable faith in a God who is eternally good shines through the pages – a God who sustains, even in the most difficult circumstances.

"My Diane" is an easy read, you will not want to put it down. The road for Diane has been far from easy, however. Through all the trauma of her childhood and teenage years when no one appeared to know or understand or even, at times, care, there was one whose loving care for her never diminished. Diane now sings and testifies of that One and the miracle that God has done is plain for all to see.

When Barbara phoned and told me the news of the final piece of the jigsaw coming into place, I told her, "It's time to write that book now." Little did I realise that I would be given the privilege of writing the foreword.

After thirty-three years Diane Ryder is now enjoying a full life and day by day the miracle of what has taken place continues to unfold. For Diane the curtain has just gone up and it is my prayer that the readers of this book will come to know the one who has made it all possible. His name is Jesus and he can become your friend and Saviour too.

God bless you, Diane. We thank God for you.

Pastor Cliff Henderson
New Life Pentecostal Church, Billingham

Dedication

This book is dedicated to my eldest daughter, Jacqueline, and my son, Paul. I want to declare my love for them because they have a special place in my heart and by writing this book about the life of their sister, Diane, it will reveal that my quest in life has been that she would be like them.

I dreamed a dream – it has now come true.

Contents

Acknowledgements		8
Introduction		9
1	The birth	11
2	Sticks and stones	21
3	Goodbye to broken dreams	31
4	The reunion	39
5	Fear has torment	49
6	The Special School	65
7	For this child have I prayed	73
8	God's way of escape	79
9	The right diagnosis	91
10	From a mother to a mother	103
11	Not a cross, a blessing	111
12	The final curtain	119

Acknowledgements

I would like to thank my dear husband, Jack, for all his love and support.

Thank you, also, to my Christian friend, Pat Grantham, who edited and typed the material contained in this book.

I am grateful to Pastor Tony Hill, Pastor Ron Smith and Pastor Cliff Henderson, whose ministries have made a significant impact in Diane's life; also in grateful memory of Pastor Maurice Boyle and evangelist, Arthur Williams.

Our sincere thanks also go to Mrs Janet Richards. Thank you for being there for Diane at a time when she needed a friend.

Introduction

After my daughter, Diane, had celebrated her twenty-first birthday party I felt a desire to write a book about her life as it was very evident to me that once again God was doing marvellous changes in her. Yet I decided to wait until she was older and pray that the picture would be complete. Little did I know that twelve years would pass before my prayer was finally answered and then I would put pen to paper.

How ironic that the day I started the book the news came on the television that Diana, Princess of Wales, had been tragically killed. I cried at the finality of this life that had been cut off. Diana, once the people's princess, only thirty-six years old, had had her life taken away.

My Diane, our little princess, aged thirty-three, had been given her life back.

Chapter 1
The birth

On our lounge wall hangs a picture of my daughter, Diane, and as I sit in my armchair I marvel at God's goodness and mercy as I look up at this lovely young woman and see a face that shows God's glory. I ask myself can this be the same girl that teenagers mocked and ridiculed?

Yet it is true. And this picture has a wonderful story to relate, of a life that was just like a jigsaw puzzle – for many years the pieces were missing, until God the Great Creator gave me the final part to make the picture complete.

Diane's eyes seem to speak out "Hey, Dad, Mam, this is how God intended me to be. I've been set free!" Yet I am also very much aware that without the Lord's intervention, it would be a very different story.

My Diane

It was in July 1964. I was pregnant with my second child. My husband, Jack, and our circle of married friends had persuaded me to book the local maternity home for the birth.

"You will be well looked after" they said. "Nothing can go wrong. You will be safe in there." I just went along with it all and kept on working in my small hairdressing salon. The customers were very loyal and assured me that they would come back after I had given birth to our baby.

One night after getting ready for bed the pains started. I knew it was time for Jack to drive me to the Home. It was only a short journey and as I got out of the car and walked up to the gates of the large Victorian building a shudder went through me and I knew that I had made one of the biggest mistakes of my life. I rang the bell and was taken into one of the many rooms by the matron who did nothing to make me feel at ease.

A midwife took me to the labour room where I was prepared for the birth. Then suddenly I was alone and the shouts and moans from faceless women made me think I was in the House of Horrors. My only comfort was the sight of the bell at the side of my bed.

But as I lay in the dimly lit room and the labour pains became more frequent I felt frightened even to call for assistance until I knew that my baby was soon

The birth

to be born. My hand came down sharp on to the bell and in minutes two midwives were at my side.

The cold manner of the senior midwife made me afraid and the pain was excruciating. I shouted out and immediately her hand came down hard across my face. "Shut up!" she said. "You have already had one child." Now I knew my fears were not unfounded. This was the House of Horrors and this was the midwife from hell.

House of Horrors

I stifled my screams and cried out to God inwardly. "Please help me. This birth is taking so long". Then it was all over. They had gone – my baby with them. Why hadn't the midwives shown me my baby? I didn't even know if I'd given birth to a boy or a girl. "Oh, never mind," I told myself. "It's 3 am. They must want me to have a good sleep." I soon drifted over into sweet oblivion.

I awoke to the sound of clattering pots and plenty of activity. Later I was transferred to a very pleasant room where, once I had made myself presentable, breakfast was served to me.

To my dismay, the senior midwife showed her face again, only now she was a different person, fawning around me. I soon found out why. My family doctor

My Diane

would shortly be coming to examine me and the midwife was afraid I would disclose what occurred earlier. But she had no cause to worry. My lips were sealed.

I heard footsteps coming down the corridor then in swept my family doctor – such a refreshing sight. Here was a professional whose bedside manner gave me comfort and sympathy for I was sure he sensed that I was not my usual self. So after he had examined me we talked about things in general, yet strangely enough my baby was not mentioned in our conversation, and I still did not know why my baby was not in my arms.

My doctor got up to leave and as I glanced at the clock I could not believe how quickly the time had passed. It would be just a couple of hours to visiting time. I lay back on my bed hoping to snatch a few minutes' sleep but my mind began to wander back to the time when Jacqueline, my first baby had been born and how different everything had been – having the birth in my own home with my own mother on hand. The best part had been that Jack, my husband, could share my joy almost immediately. I chuckled to myself remembering that it was only three months later, and to everyone's amusement, that I was sitting holding my mother's hand as she gave birth to my sister, Judith! Then a thought suddenly occurred to me that because Jacqueline was being looked after by my fa-

The birth

ther and mother, Judith, my very young sister, would be playing with Jacqueline and this would distract her from missing me.

I shook myself out of my daydreaming and began to freshen myself up. To my delight in walked one of the midwives with my baby. As she was placed in my arms I thought how lovely she looked with her black hair and round face and I could hardly wait for Jack to come and see his little daughter.

The time seemed to pass very quickly and soon Jack came into the room and greeted me with a tender embrace. Oh how I needed that! I had begun to feel depressed thinking that I was to spend ten days alone in the place. Never mind! I would cherish the short time with my husband and see what he thought of our baby.

What's wrong with her nose?

"Well, what do you think of her?" I asked him, my heart bursting with pride.

"What's wrong with her nose? It looks broken," he replied. My heart sank as I fought back the tears. I could not believe he had said that. Jack quickly changed the subject, realising his lack of sensitivity.

We both agreed that our baby would be called Diane and then he gave me all the news about

My Diane

Jacqueline, our home, and the clients who were asking about me and enquiring when the salon would be reopening. I told Jack hairdressing was the last thing on my mind and it would have to be a few weeks before I would be able to start work again. Then it was time for Jack to leave.

As I settled down for another lonely night I wondered what tomorrow would bring. The next morning I was pleasantly surprised to have the company of a young woman in the bed next to me. She had given birth to a baby boy. She was still drowsy and it would be some time before we could have a conversation. I had to be patient but the time seemed to drag. Even the ticking of the clock seemed to irritate me. Worrying thoughts kept nagging at me. Diane had hardly suckled at my breast, content to stay in a deep sleep most of the time.

I glanced towards my room mate whose eyes looked enormous as she returned my gaze. It was obvious she did not know where she was. I gave her a warm smile and introduced myself. She told me her name was Moira Strachan and explained that she had been drugged up to the eyeballs. However, she had been shown kindness by her midwives who had given her gas and air. When I shared my experience she was shocked.

If she thought I was being over sensitive regard-

The birth

ing my treatment at the hands of those midwives she was soon to see it for herself. As I was doubled up with severe after birth pains, my plea for pain killers was ignored. I recall Moira was the only one to comfort me. It seemed like the school of hard knocks was to be my portion.

The glorious day arrives

It was time for us to mix with the other inmates – whoops, sorry, just a slip of the tongue – I meant to say the other young mothers and their babies. Yet honestly with all the rules and regulations one could be forgiven for thinking it was like being under house arrest because if you went down on bended knees asking to go home early it would be refused. Ten days was the sentence – no more, no less.

Finally the glorious day arrived. I was to be discharged - what a relief! My case was packed in record time and I went round everyone to say goodbye. I hugged Moira expecting never to see her again. Little did I know that our paths would cross in a remarkable way.

Then, the moment I had been longing for, Jack brought Jacqueline into the room. As she flung herself into my outstretched arms I broke down sobbing uncontrollably. Our little girl seemed so grown up in

My Diane

such a short time. As I picked up Diane and Jack gathered together my belongings we stepped out into the welcoming fresh air. A thought flashed through my mind. I came in here like a young girl and I was leaving as a woman. Little did I know that ahead of me there would be a river of tears to be shed and a fiery furnace to withstand.

Chapter 2

Sticks and stones

Once we were in the car and on our way home all thoughts of the maternity home faded from my mind. I was excited that we would be together again as a family. As soon as the car stopped we quickly rushed inside our neat three-bedroomed house. It looked so cosy and clean and the coal fire seemed to be so welcoming. It felt good to be home. I inspected my salon which was situated at the front part of the house and a part of me wanted to start work as soon as possible.

That day would come round quickly. The salon re-opened and I knew that news would get round that it was business as usual. True to their word my clients returned to me. My mother, who was also a hairdresser, helped me and a young woman called Carol worked for me. It was a happy and friendly place. Jacqueline

My Diane

and Judith kept the clients entertained and Diane was no trouble at all because she was always asleep.

Recalling the first time I showed Diane to the customers, one lady took one look and exclaimed "Oh look at her eyes, they're so dull." No one said Diane was lovely. They just turned away. I was bewildered. "My baby is lovely," I said to myself.

Yet as the days turned to weeks something began to trouble me. Diane would sleep for hours on end and the short time she was awake she never moved or showed any interest in me or her surroundings, neither did she cry. My eyes would stray to her nose and I began to agree with Jack that her nose was broken.

When I voiced my fears to the health visitors they just laughed at me. "Be thankful," they said. "You've got a very placid baby. Don't compare her with Jacqueline. All children are not the same." So I tried to be thankful for my contented baby and continued working until one day I recall an incident that filled my heart with fear. I was perming a client's hair and had to go and check that Diane was all right. I mentioned to this lady that Diane had slept for eight hours and I could not wake her up. "Bring her to me," she said. "I'm a nurse." I quickly brought Diane to her. She prized open her eyelids.

"Get a doctor immediately!" said the nurse. As I moved to the door Jack walked in and with a loud

Sticks and stones

voice said "Hello, Diane!" and at that very moment her eyes opened wide.

Full of apologies the nurse said she had made a mistake. Yet though I was relieved I felt it was a warning that all was not well and from that moment I started to watch Diane more closely than ever.

Dull and lifeless

The health visitors still insisted that I must not compare her with Jacqueline but I could not help it. My first born had walked and talked well before other babies. Her large beautiful eyes were as bright as buttons and everyone said that she was lovely. I could see that by contrast Diane was plain, her eyes were dull and her lifeless – demeanour which would later invoke verbal abuse, especially from other children.

I felt so sad for our little one and yet I knew that even I had very little love for her. There was no bonding at all, until the day an incident occurred which changed everything. A customer had asked to use the bathroom and as she passed Diane I heard her say, "Come here you fat, ugly-looking beast!" I made a sound and the woman turned round. She knew I had heard her cruel remark but I showed no reaction for she had done Diane a good turn. From that moment, I had bonded with my baby.

My Diane

A wonderful surge of mother love swept through me. I was proud that she was my Diane and in my heart I knew these 'stonings' would not be allowed in her direction for much longer. A plan was forming in my mind of how I could protect her.

When I was a child there was a little rhyme, "Sticks and stones may break my bones but calling cannot hurt me." This is only a half-truth as a stone may wound the body but words can wound within. Words are very powerful and can pierce like a sword. Diane was verbally abused from birth but it couldn't affect her if I absorbed the insults and insensitive remarks.

I bought a child's seat which was placed on Diane's pram. When I went out shopping Jacqueline sat on the seat and Diane was laid flat in the pram with the covers over her. We would walk a little way then friends and neighbours would stop to talk. After a few minutes the conversation would centre around Jacqueline's progress. Then they would lift the covers to look at Diane and, without exception, they would enquire how she was doing. "Fine!" I would reply, then hurry away.

Shopping became very stressful and I have a vivid memory of visiting an exclusive baby shop. My two girls were with me and my little sister, Judith. After treating the two girls to lovely coat-and-hat sets I asked

Sticks and stones

the middle-aged owner to show me some coats for Diane. With a look of contempt and a wave of her hand she said "Oh, don't bother paying much for her clothes. Get something cheap." With a firm voice I replied, "She will get the same as they get!" How thankful I was that I had shown self-control.

From that day I began to notice other babies, especially when I took Diane to the baby clinic. The other mothers would be chatting away telling each other how quick their babies were, how advanced for their age. I had to agree with them. They were wonderful – babies of six months sitting up and looking so bright and alert. How glad I was Diane was asleep. This was my excuse to make my escape and the short journey home was always with tears and a heavy heart. I was troubled with questions and there was no one to give me answers, not even the staff at the clinic.

God, please help me!

My mind was in a turmoil. I cried out, "God, please help me!" But then my mind would say,"Why should he? Four years ago you walked away from him." Yes, that was true. I had been brought up in a Christian home from the age of five, always going to church, having parents that believed in prayer. I had wanted to run away from all that. I had felt that God

My Diane

wasn't real to me, as he was to my parents.

The sound of the doorbell brought me out of my despondency. I opened the door and was surprised to see Pastor Boyle, the minister of our local church where my family still attended. I glanced down at the floor feeling embarrassed. Then I realised that he could not see me, remembering that he had suddenly lost his sight about two years previously.

"May I come in?" the pastor asked.

"Of course" I answered politely, leading him down the hall into the lounge and guiding him round the furniture.

As he made himself comfortable my mind was running riot. "Why is he here?" I asked myself. "Is he going to try to persuade me to come back to church? My mother must have asked him to visit me but it won't work. I'm all right as I am."

As if he could read my mind, Pastor Boyle quickly came to the point. Would Jack and I like to have Diane dedicated to the Lord, thanking him for her safe delivery? That was the invitation, take it or leave it. There was no pushing or persuasion. After about half an hour he got up to leave and I must admit it was too soon for me because his presence and conversation had had a calming effect on my troubled mind.

As I closed the door after him I realised I was warming to the idea of a special occasion. My mind

Sticks and stones

began to race. How many sandwiches would I need? The cakes and pies should be baked well in advance. The girls would need new dresses – that's if Jack agreed with it all.

Preparing the evening meal that night, there was a lightness in my heart for the first time in months. I couldn't wait for Jack to come home from work. My sister, Pam, was helping with the girls and when my husband arrived home he must have thought he was in the wrong house, I was so calm and happy. After our meal, Pastor Boyle's invitation came casually into the conversation and, to my surprise, Jack agreed.

I still felt uneasy

The day arrived for all our family to meet at the church. As the service commenced the singing was beautiful and from his heart Pastor Boyle gave a fine sermon. When he dedicated Diane to God I must confess it was very moving. At the end of the service all our friends gathered around us and we felt very welcome. Yet I still felt uneasy because I did not want to come back to the Church.

I felt relieved when, later on, my parents and family members returned to our home where a lovely buffet was waiting for them.

After the dedication I just dropped back into my

My Diane

old routine. I never found time even to pray and Diane was getting worse. One weekend I paid a visit to my parents' home. My attitude that day was one of self pity and my mam and I had words, after which I stormed out of her home in anger. "No one understands what I'm going through," I said to myself. But by the time I reached home I was beginning to feel guilty for upsetting my mother. As I opened the front door I felt so confused. What should I do? Go back and apologise or go to church and get myself put right? Glancing at the clock I knew there was an hour before the service began. Quickly getting the girls ready for bed and leaving Jack in charge, I dashed through the streets to the Pentecostal Church to be met with the melodious sound of gospel music. The words 'Amazing grace, how sweet the sound that saved a wretch like me,' a song I knew so well, met me as I entered the building.

As I took my seat I felt like the prodigal son returning to his father. I don't remember much of the service except that when the lay preacher expounded the word of God my heart felt as if it was being torn apart. I fought back the tears and tried to ignore the still, quiet voice of the Lord: "Behold I stand at the door and knock." Soon the tears ran down my cheeks and I began to sob, oblivious to the rest of the congregation. There was a battle raging within me and I was

Sticks and stones

unable to deal with it. Jumping up from my seat, I made my way to the door but the lay preacher was there to meet me. Taking hold of my hand he said gently, "Go home and tell God all about it." I thanked him and, walking out into the night air, I made a conscious decision. I needed to lay my burden down at the foot of the cross. I was desperate to get home and be alone with my Creator

I knew He was real

Reaching home I ran upstairs to our bedroom and, dropping to my knees, I found words pouring from my mouth. "God, if you really exist, take my life. Come into my heart. Cleanse me from all my sin. From this night on I want to serve you. Thank you for your son, Jesus Christ, and what He did for me on the cross." I was just twenty-four but I meant every word. Instantly God's love and presence swept over me and that night I knew He was real.

At bedtime I drifted into a restful sleep. Next morning I awoke to the sound of birds singing and instantly my thoughts turned to the events of the previous night. Had it been pure emotion, I asked myself? Closing my eyes and offering up a secret prayer (as Jack was in the bedroom and I had not told him of the previous night's events), that same peace and love

My Diane

came over me and I was so glad to be alive. The world seemed different now.

I waited for a suitable opportunity to share with my husband what the Lord had done for me but when I told him he soon brought me down to earth. "I'll give you six weeks, then you'll be back to normal," he laughed. Feeling a little deflated I picked up my Bible and read John's gospel, Chapter 3, v16. That was enough for me. God loved me and He would keep me going on by His power. Whatever lay ahead the Lord Jesus would be with me. His timing had been perfect and my surrender had been vital for His plans regarding my life and Diane's. Prayer and faith, together with much patience, would be my close companions from now on.

Chapter 3

Goodbye to broken dreams

The events of the next few months are mostly a blur except for the moment when I finally accepted that there was something drastically wrong with Diane. Her back was very arched and she was not able to sit up. She never smiled, her eyes never followed us; she showed no recognition of me or any member of the family, which was most distressing. Even her little sister, Jacqueline, could not get her to respond. Nothing we did could stimulate our baby.

Jack and I sat down to have a serious discussion about the best course of action and we agreed Diane must be seen by our family doctor. I remember so clearly walking into the surgery and pouring out my fears to our doctor. I remember how he took her from my arms and placed her on the floor and I watched as

My Diane

she fell to one side. He repeated this procedure many times but to no avail. Shaking his head he told me Diane would have to be fitted with a steel corset and that in his opinion there was definitely something wrong with her back. He told me that he would write to the paediatrician and I would be given a date to see him.

In a daze I thanked him for his kindness and closed the surgery door. As I walked slowly home, the weight of the world seemed to be on my shoulders. Arriving home I felt somehow the house had lost its warmth. As I stepped inside it seemed as if it was mocking me. My mind was in a turmoil as I opened the door of the hairdressing salon. Negative thoughts pervaded my mind. "This is your worst nightmare come true," I said to myself. "The shop will have to go. It was once your dream but Diane will need all your time now. You never thought this could happen to you, Barbara."

I cried out "Stop! You negative thoughts, I refuse to entertain you!" Then once again I was on my knees in prayer to God, asking Him to heal my baby. Opening my Bible, the verse "They that believe shall lay hands on the sick and they shall recover" seemed to set my heart free from any unbelief and I knew that faith was beginning to rise up within me. I felt upheld by my family and by a mother who believed in prayer. My brother, John, and sister, Pam, always helped me

Goodbye to broken dreams

in practical ways. With all this love I was finding strength to carry on. But it was God's power that I needed at this present time. There was no change in Diane, yet there was certainly a change in me – I was looking to God for a miracle.

They that believe...

I recall the wonderful day when the faith of God was so much in my heart that I put my hands on Diane and prayed in the name of the Lord Jesus Christ, according to the promise in His word: "They that believe ..." that was *me*, "Lord I believe nothing is impossible with You. Thank You for healing her back."

It was done! The assurance that God had worked a miracle brought great peace upon my life. Diane could now sit up! She began to reach for her toys. The first piece of the jigsaw puzzle had been given to me.

I was elated; there was such a spring in my step and my work in the hair salon was much more interesting now that Diane was able to sit in a high chair and watch us all. The ladies took a great interest in her and I told them what God had done. I looked forward to her showing progress like any normal baby.

Her first birthday passed and the months went by quickly until she was near to celebrating her second

My Diane

birthday, when, for the second time, I knew the battle was not over. Still she could not smile and her legs were so weak it was impossible for her to stand. Many times I stood her up against the wall only for her to fall like a rag doll when I let go. I once stood her against the settee for a photograph and she leant forward as if her back had a hump on it Diane never crawled like a normal child.. Again I was in a dilemma. Did I have to accept defeat from this giant that was attacking me, or should I ask God again for help? After much prayer I knew the Lord was going to heal Diane.

One lovely day in July 1966 near to her birthday I paid mam and dad a visit. My sister-in-law, Jan Banks, had also had the same idea. Jane was happily licking an ice cream cornet and Diane's lips were longing for some. I stood her against the wall and prayed fervently in the name of the Lord Jesus. Jan held out the cornet and as I said "Lord fill these legs with your mighty power," Diane took three steps. Oh! The joy in our hearts in that precious moment! No money or gifts could have thrilled us like this second piece of the jigsaw. Yet my joy was short lived because I knew more heartache was to come.

Our friends and neighbours were astounded as Diane walked towards them. They all give their opinion – she was just late in her development. Yet I could sense there was a formidable force waiting to make

Goodbye to broken dreams

me surrender, demanding me to look and see what would be inevitable. Never would I allow myself to view Diane's condition pessimistically because my eyes were looking up to a God who encourages us to have faith in what we do not see, believing that our faith will be rewarded.

Out of our hands

Once again Jack and I had decisions to make and as we sat around the fire drinking endless cups of coffee we decided the house would have to go on the market, yet we felt it wasn't quite the time. Maybe we would wait another year before contacting an estate agent. However, three months later it was all taken out of our hands. I found I was pregnant again. Jack and I were delighted and we discussed the possibility of my giving birth to a baby boy. Thus we decided to set the wheels in motion for our home to be put on the market.

That night sleep was impossible. The thought of telling my clients that the hair salon would be closed in three month's time turned my stomach over. I knew how they loved coming to have their hair done. They confided in me and always felt relaxed with my mother who would try to help them with their problems. My mind raced. What about Carol Heath? She would be

My Diane

upset at losing her job. How would I manage three children? What if we could not sell the house? Tossing and turning, my turbulent thoughts continued until the crack of dawn.

How I welcomed that new day despite my worries of the previous night. My mind was made up. I must be strong and get on with the task ahead of me. Finding a strength that I never knew before, I started to put words into action. When my ladies were informed of my intentions they accepted the situation and wished me well in my new beginning.

Everything now seemed to be moving at great speed. Our home had been sold and our house-hunting was at last at an end. Jack and I had both agreed that the last house we viewed was ideal for us. We would be able to simply move in. Everything was spotless and because by then I was six months pregnant, this suited us very well – we didn't want to have to start decorating. I was beginning to see the Lord was helping me and although we were leaving friends and neighbours I knew God would be with me as always. He would be a friend that I could never lose.

Departure day came with endless boxes filled with toys, clothes and pots; our home scrubbed spotless; the rooms filled with helpers. My sister, Pam, sorting out the children, including little Judith. Jack keeping busy doing last minute jobs. Then the sound of the

Goodbye to broken dreams

large removal van. I watched with mixed emotions as the rooms were emptied one by one. As I was the last one to leave, turning round with tears filling my eyes my heart seemed to cry out, "Goodbye to broken dreams, I'm leaving here with losses, but there *is* a bright tomorrow ahead."

My Diane

Chapter 4
The reunion

Arriving at our new home, Jack and I were pleasantly surprised as the previous owners had left every room immaculate. We glanced at each other, then down at the many boxes which would have to be unpacked. Now all we needed were some more hands to make light work of it all.

By midday the house was filled with family and friends. Laughter and fun was heard coming from all the rooms as we frantically worked to put everything in its place before nightfall.

Jack's mum made sure there was a constant supply of scones, sandwiches and tea. Thirsty workers kept coming to the kitchen with empty mugs to be refilled, then gradually some sort of order was taking place.

My Diane

Once our furniture was installed, beds and curtains put up, it was beginning to look more like home to us. Finally, as the last picture was put on the wall and family and friends had departed, we sat down, satisfied we had made a good move.

That night, as I bathed the girls and put them to bed, I started to count my blessings, thanking God for our health. I gave thanks for my husband who loved me; for the gift of our two children and also the little one still in my womb. What more could I want?

Yet peace was to elude me once again. Another trial was shortly to come my way bringing trouble and hostility to all of us.

The first few weeks passed without any problems. I felt revitalised as preparations for the birth of our baby were underway; the midwife was booked and delivery would take place in our new home. Wild horses would not drag me down the road I had previously taken. Diane was now getting stronger yet she could not speak one word. This was something that I refused to face until after my delivery.

The wonderful day arrived when a beautiful baby boy was placed in my arms. Just to see Jack's face made me feel so fulfilled. Our little one would bring such joy to us. Our minds would be taken off Diane a little. Sadly, we soon found out there was to be no respite, for now I had two babies to look after. Diane

The reunion

was becoming very hard work.

Realisation dawned that I could not live behind closed doors and keep Jacqueline inside the house for hours. So on strict instructions to Jacqueline to keep her eye on Diane, I allowed them out of the back door to play with the other children. For a short while everything seemed fine then pandemonium set in. Jacqueline came in crying that the children were calling Diane 'mental' and one of the mothers said her two girls would not be allowed to play with her. True to her word the children were never seen again in the back street and their house went up for sale. We had 'lowered the tone' of the road by moving in, or so we were told. My tears were many and bitter that night. My pride had taken a beating. We had been made to feel like scum. Even the Lord seemed as if He was not answering my prayer.

More and more despondent

No one wanted to know my little girl and gradually I was becoming more and more despondent with the stress of living through this heartache. A few doors from our home was a little corner shop which became a godsend to me. I could meet people and talk to them and we made lots of friends and, sadly, a few enemies also.

My Diane

No matter how hard I tried to shield Diane from trouble it seemed to follow her. I recall one morning making my way to the shop and Diane running ahead of me. An older child, oblivious to me, put her face right in front of Diane's and said "You're daft and mental!"

"How long was this to go on?" I asked God. "Is there no joy to come into my life?" He showed me that night that I was still walking in His will, despite the hardness of the way.

It was Friday – prayer meeting time – and after calling for mum we both walked the short distance to church relishing the escape from the old routine. As I entered the church I gazed round the hall where just about twenty people were gathered. I froze in disbelief as I spotted my room mate from the nursing home, Moira Strachan. Patiently I waited for the service to end, not being able to concentrate on the meeting for wandering thoughts. I made my way over to Moira and I will always remember the look of pure joy on her face as we met and hugged one another. It was an emotional reunion and from that moment we became close friends.

From that night Moira came frequently to our home. We would share our experiences. She understood my heart and prayed with me and shared some of the load. I remember one day Moira called to have

The reunion

a coffee with me. Mum also called in and we were having a chat about our families. Suddenly Diane fell to the floor moaning as if she was in agony. Her hands and feet were twisting and writhing in agony. Her eyes were full of fear. We all prayed and suddenly it stopped. "What was that?" I said. Mum replied, "Well, it wasn't a fit." We checked to see if she had been affected by it but she seemed all right. Soon after, though, she had another attack. I prayed again for Diane and she never had another recurrence. It was nearly thirty years later before I found out what actually happened.

Diane was still not talking

During the next few months I felt stretched to the limit. Diane was taken back to the doctors, then two appointments were made to visit the paediatrician as Diane was still not talking.

While my sister took care of Jacqueline and baby Paul my task was to try to teach Diane. Endlessly my finger would point to the various parts of her face and body: eyes, nose, ears, teeth, hoping and praying that some of it would be understood. Taking her to the experts left me even more confused as no diagnosis was ever pronounced.

Moira and the other young mothers were starting

My Diane

to prepare to send their children to mainstream school, which was very close to our home. Jack and I were in a dilemma as to what to do. We knew there was a possibility the headmistress might not accept Diane into her school.

I knew what would bring me peace and direction: God's word and praying "Father God, show me the next step to take." As I opened the Bible to the book of James, Chapter 2 v 17 it read: "Faith without works is dead." Taking this as God speaking through His word, I realised action was needed and the Lord would sustain me. I shared with my family the next step I would take and they agreed it was best for Diane.

One day as I sat in the armchair, feeling low in my spirit, I felt the same welling-up within me of God's presence. I asked the Lord to give me a sign that if Diane could write her name before she was due to go to school, I would know my decision was right.

Spending hours going over her name I waited for her to copy it. There was much frustration in the weeks that followed but my persistence paid off. Diane began to write her full name and address. We were all elated. I bought new clothes for her, gave her hair a light perm and she looked lovely. She had by now lost weight and to us she seemed no different from the other children. Nothing stood in our way regarding her starting school. The head teacher agreed to let

The reunion

Diane start the new term, even though she was still not speaking.

The wonderful day arrived when, with all the mums, the little ones were lead into the classroom. There were plenty of tears, yet I came back home rejoicing that at last I was going to have some time for my other two children, though Paul, thank God, was coming on in leaps and bounds. He was walking and forming words and was such a happy child, we doted on him. Jacqueline and Judith were doing well at the school that Diane had just started; they were known as the 'terrible twins'. Life now seemed a little more relaxed; in fact it seemed to be falling into a pleasant routine.

The end of the world

I made friends with a few of the neighbours, a young woman called Kath Stokes often called to have a coffee with me. She was mother to six beautiful children and they would sometimes play with my girls. This brought me great delight. Moira was also a regular visitor to our home. We attended church as often as possible and she would share with us about the day she found God. It was a unique testimony, one which I could visualise for I, too, could recall that day when the sky suddenly turned black. Many people had

My Diane

thought it could be the end of the world. Moira had believed it was and began to pray, calling on God to forgive her and putting her house in order. She vowed to find a church to worship in if it wasn't the end of the world.

The horrible blackness lifted about lunch time. Mothers were able to collect their children from school. It was quite a talking point for days, yet this experience had amazingly brought my friend into my path again and that friendship would continue for thirty-four years. Moira would see the wonderful power of God transforming my helpless baby into a life that would shine in this vicinity.

Sadly, Jack and I never felt a sense of peace in our home and we would often day dream of moving house again. It seemed to us that we were destined to live there for years but little did we know that about two years later we would be on the move again – for the third time.

It so happened that my parents called to tell us about a beautiful semi-detached house that was for sale. As I prepared lunch for them mother explained that her garden looked onto the garden of the semi. "We could have a way made through with a gate!" said mother. The expression on my face must have been hilarious because everyone burst out laughing. Ignoring it I blurted out, "I wish it was possible." Then

The reunion

I proceeded to ask my father the price. "Over £3,000," replied dad, then adding quickly "It's in lovely condition." "Way out of our reach," I thought, "yet it's worth discussing it with Jack; circumstances could change."

Later that night, once the children were settled in bed, Jack and I talked for hours on the possibility of us moving once again. The thought of a large private garden where the children would be able to play without anyone bothering them and Diane would be left in peace, was very appealing. It would be our dream home – a new beginning. How could I have known that ten years of intense misery and unhappiness lay ahead? The time passed quickly, the mortgage was granted and at last we were making preparations to move into our semi-detached dream home.

My Diane

Chapter 5

Fear has torment

As my husband turned the key to open the door of our new house I couldn't help but compare it with our previous home. Everything in here was so perfect; the decor was expensive looking and I knew the professionals had done all the decorating. The carpets were thick and luxurious and as I looked out through the enormous picture window our three children were playing happily in the garden. Turning to Jack I said, "We must buy a slide and swing for Christmas for them." Putting his arm around my waist he said, "Yes, that's a good idea. They'll love a slide." Just at that moment I felt I hadn't a care in the world. No one knew Diane or any of our family in this crescent and we would keep ourselves to ourselves, though we would be polite.

My Diane

Dad was starting to make a way through our two gardens. What more could we want? But the feeling of Utopia was soon to be dispelled. Never could I have imagined the fear and torment that was waiting outside of our peaceful home. Diane and I would soon feel the force of its fury. Only my faith in God stopped me from being crushed. We experienced just one week of peace before cruel tongues began to wag.

One morning I opened the front door to collect the milk off the step. My neighbour had the same idea and, as our eyes met, I gave her a warm smile and began, "Good morning, it's a lovely..." but my voice trailed off as I saw her stony stare. She closed the door without a word. I was stung by her reaction. "Why this treatment? She doesn't know me and I have never seen her before in my life. "Oh, never mind, she'll come round in time," I thought.

Later that day as I collected the two girls from school the lady from across the road gave me the same look of contempt when I tried to be friendly. When Jack came home from work we discussed this strange attitude from the neighbours. "You must have imagined it, Barbara," my husband said.

By the end of the week all was to be revealed. As I took the children to school a lady came to speak to me and she explained that the people in the crescent had been warned about me. Apparently I had been

Fear has torment

given the cold shoulder because I had dared to move in to their domain with a mentally retarded child. They had been told to keep their gates locked to keep her out.

I couldn't wait to get home to sob my heart out to God in prayer. I knew what that woman had said was true because I knew there were women living near the crescent who were against Diane and wanted to torment us.

Confirming my suspicions

To confirm my suspicions two little girls appeared in our garden one day. I think it was the children's voices that had attracted them. I asked them to come and play with Diane but they replied "No, our mum has told us not to play with the girl that can't talk." As I told the girls to leave the garden and go home I asked myself "Why? Why has it got to be like this?"

Desperately seeking an answer I called on a lady I knew who had a severely disabled child. She was an inspiration to me as she seemed very strong and able to shrug off the contemptuous attitudes of those around her. I asked her to tell me her secret of how to survive the cruel remarks and stares of ignorant people. She told me to harden myself; to stop crying and lift my head up and remember that there, but for the grace of

My Diane

God, go those tormentors. It could have happened to them. This helped me a lot because I realised I had the fear of man and would have to overcome it.

The months passed by. The slide and swing were duly installed, courtesy of my mother-in-law, and the children's excited voices, as they played, filled the garden. However, six months later we had to sell the equipment as our neighbour complained at the noise. "Oh, Jack," I sobbed "is there ever going to be any light in this darkness?"

One morning brought a pleasant surprise: it was an invitation to have a week's holiday with the church down in Bognor Regis. Apparently a major conference was to be held there. It was the Assembly of God Pentecostal Church's conference where some very prominent speakers and evangelists would be taking part and would be praying for the sick. My brother, John, and his wife had called to tell us and they persuaded Jack to come along with us.

At last my mind had something new to think about. We could hardly wait for the day of departure to get away for the much-needed break. The coach journey was fun and the company very friendly. Our children slept most of the time and Jack and I contentedly snuggled together, determined not to let anything spoil our holiday.

Arriving at our destination I had never imagined

Fear has torment

there would be so many people. It seemed hundreds of them were hurrying past us with their large suitcases. We were amused at the sight as it was still early morning, yet they were so joyful and there was an air of expectancy that filled the whole place.

"Your little girl needs prayer."

The first few days were perfect. The children were no trouble to us at all. The food was good and the pastors provided us with excellent preaching at the evening meetings. All was well until the day I went swimming in the pool. Jack was holding Diane in his arms when suddenly she started to cry and became so distraught I had to come out of the water. A pastor came over to us and said, "Your little girl needs prayer. She can't speak or communicate. I'll get someone to come to your chalet."

As we returned to our room Diane was falling asleep. As I laid her on the bed there was a faint knock on the door. When Jack opened it I could hardly believe my eyes: standing in the doorway was Pastor Gerald Chamberlain and the well-known evangelist, Arthur Williams. "Come in," I stammered. Arthur walked over to Diane, prayed for her and then said: "The Lord is healing your child but it is going to be gradual." This was great news and made sense be-

My Diane

cause God had already worked miraculously on her body; it was her speech that now needed to be brought out.

The rest of the week passed without event and then our holiday came to an end. We were returning home and I felt more positive towards the unavoidable experiences of life with Diane, though I knew in my heart there was much more trouble to come. As we got off the coach near our home all we could think of was our comfortable bed and a hot cup of Horlicks. Tomorrow would take care of itself.

We woke up to a beautiful day. The sun was shining brightly and the birds were singing, it was good to be alive. I felt that nothing was going to let me down that day. Quickly the two girls were made ready for school. Breakfast was just toast and cereal and after walking the girls to the gates of their school I took Paul into town with me. We spent a couple of hours around town and then returned home for lunch. Just a lovely day, I thought. Yet in less than one hour my world was torn apart.

The door bell rang and as I went to answer it I was surprised to find Diane holding the hand of a young woman not much older than myself. "May I come in?" she asked, stepping into the hallway. "I'm the school's medical officer and I've come to inform you that your child is severely mentally retarded and

Fear has torment

will have to be taken out of mainstream school."

I felt the blood drain from my face as I stared at her in disbelief. "No, you're wrong. It's only her speech that's hindering her," I heard myself say. I will never forget her look of coldness and her manner which was void of any compassion as she repeated that Diane would have to go to the local training centre and that she would only get worse. She turned around to leave, saying, "I've made an appointment for you to see the educational psychologist, and also the head teacher would like a word with you." With that she was gone, leaving me in total shock.

Holding back tears

Waiting for my husband to return home from work I dreaded having to tell him all the details about Diane's assessment from school and how they were determined to get her out. I tried to look cheerful as he walked into the kitchen but he soon realised I was holding back tears. Taking me into the lounge, he sat me down and we talked over the events of the day. The colour drained from his face as he looked at me in disbelief. "Don't worry," I said, "there is still the educational psychologist to see and she might prove them wrong." Jack looked relieved that all might not be lost. Yet I found myself wondering what tomorrow

My Diane

would bring. Would this woman bring us hope or despair?

The morning of Diane's appointment I remember so clearly: the feeling of nausea and being slightly afraid of what was soon to take place. As Diane and I entered the old building with its drab-looking walls I was dreading the office door opening and glimpsing this person who could hammer the final nail into Diane's coffin. Giving a weak knock on her door I waited with bated breath. "Come in!" spoke an abrupt voice. As we entered the middle-aged woman instantly reduced me to a nervous wreck. She never smiled once and Diane, she said, would have to be interviewed alone. "You will distract her," she said. As she showed me out of her office I looked back at my daughter. She looked terrified and her eyes were blinking nervously. My heart sank. I already knew what the outcome would be.

The time seemed to drag and I was becoming anxious when the office door burst open and a very angry woman, dragging Diane behind her, said "Take her away. She is a cabbage. She has no IQ at all. I will recommend that she is sent to the local training centre for severely mentally handicapped children." Then we were dismissed.

Feeling like the lowest of the low I slowly made my way home telling myself, "That's final; they've

Fear has torment

just written my daughter off. I'll visit the Headmistress and hear what she has to say."

Going through the school gates I was prepared for the encounter. It was apparent from the headmistress's conversation she had no time for Diane and wanted her removed from her school. She said they had been watching how she walked and then she proceeded to demonstrate. How I found the strength to get up and open the door I will never know for the feeling of wanting to pass out was overwhelming. I knew that floods of tears were ready to flow but to break down in front of this woman would be humiliating. Making a rapid exit I ran into the school yard sobbing. I was wretched and broken. All along the main road passers-by stared at me. I was not concerned. All I wanted to do was to get back to the sanctuary of my own home.

The final decision

Reaching out with the key to open the front door my hand was shaking. I could not believe what was happening to us. Also the thought of Jack coming home to this news was unbearable. Once inside my home and sitting with a cup of coffee my thoughts began to settle as I waited to share with my husband the final decision of the school authorities. It was a

My Diane

relief to hear his footsteps coming up the drive and as the door opened he was asking the result of Diane's test. Seeing my face he guessed that all hope was now gone. I will never forget what happened next. As I told Jack what the psychologist had said he completely broke down, sobbing. That tore at my heart, then I also broke down. We sat together completely devastated. It was as if we had just lost Diane and were grieving. We sat for a while then I collected the children from my parents' home.

As I talked things over with my father it helped me to come to terms with the inevitable and all that was left was for the experts to decide which school Diane would have to attend.

Even as Jack and I accepted the situation we would not discuss our predicament with many people as we knew it would give our neighbours more bullets to fire. They were already opposed to Diane living in their neighbourhood and it seemed that whenever we ventured outside the house there was trouble waiting for us.

I recall one day a neighbour beckoned me over to her. "Oh, how nice," I thought. "At last she's going to speak." As she opened her mouth the venom began to pour out. Pointing her finger at me she snarled, "You've made this road like this. Send your kids to the park to play. I'm not moving from here because of

Fear has torment

you. Also we don't want your God!"

For a moment I was speechless yet 'persecution' was the word that was spinning round in my head. My faith in the Creator was obviously getting to her.

Nasty lies were being told

We soon found out other nasty lies were being told. Apparently I was a medium and held seances in my home. Of course I realised that when they had seen some friends coming to my home to have their hair done they had put their own interpretation on it. How I prayed to God about those lies!

Early one morning I awoke with once again the faith of God rising up within me. "No", I told myself "this is not going to drag me down. I will not accept Diane's report." Singing at the top of my voice I went through the old hymns: The Old Rugged Cross; What a Friend We Have In Jesus. Opening the window the sound of my voice drifted out, strong and firm. When I stopped, to my amazement I could hear the sound of a piano being played and to my delight the hymns I had been singing were coming through the walls of my next door neighbour's. The Lord had answered my prayer without confrontation.

Yet still the verbal abuse continued. Diane was made a target by the other children who were torment-

My Diane

ing her. She would come in and bury her head in a cushion and sob. The children would run towards her as if they were going to play with her then run back to their gardens and hide from her. This bewildered Diane and caused her much frustration.

Jack bought her a three-wheeled bicycle to compensate for having parted with the slide and swing. How thrilled we were when she learnt how to ride it. Even this brought more pain for us for I remember the day she went round the far end of the crescent on her bike and an older girl was waiting for her with a large Alsatian. She promptly set the dog on Diane. That cruel act was to put fear into my daughter that would torment her for years. The screams from Diane were ear piercing and her heart was racing. How I calmed her down is just a blur now. My worry was that Diane would develop a phobia about dogs. We were soon to see that fear realised for when she saw any dog she froze to the spot and couldn't move. I had to carry her even as she got older and heavier.

As her mother I felt outrage at what was coming against my child. If only I could have perceived that this was only the beginning.

One morning, being in a pensive mood, I didn't hear the door bell ring or the footsteps down the hall. Hearing the sound of a familiar voice coming from the door I was glad to welcome our pastor, Tony Hill,

Fear has torment

who had come to inform me that he would like to call the church to have an all-night prayer meeting for Diane and would that be all right with Jack and I? I thanked him with tears falling down my face. Now I knew others were giving us love and support.

Rapid answers to prayer

That prayer meeting was not in vain and we will always be grateful for the group of faithful members of our church who called on the Lord to intervene. That week we saw rapid answers to our prayers. Our home was visited by Councillor Stephen Smailes who had called at the invitation of my father. He observed Diane, looked at her pages of writing and left us determined to fight for her. Next we had a visit from Mr Bob Jones who was a headmaster. His parents had asked him to come and assess her. It would be twenty-six years later that it would be revealed what his diagnosis had been; even this came at the right time.

Next came the opportunity to go to a church in Shildon where, to our surprise, the same evangelist that had prayed for Diane at the conference was going to be praying for the sick at this service not many miles from our home. As we all set off to go to the church I believed God was going to work in Diane's life again and it was her speech that needed to be

My Diane

healed. Arthur Williams prayed for many people that night: a lady who had been confined to a wheelchair walked away healed by the Lord Jesus; many more were also made whole. He came over to Diane, laid his hands on her and prayed in the name of the Lord Jesus. Then he said to me: "Tomorrow she will begin to speak." That night my family came home rejoicing at the goodness of God.

The next morning I awoke expecting a miracle and by late afternoon Diane was saying a few words, though it sounded like a young child's voice. When Jack returned home from work he was thrilled to hear her.

Our doctor then began to take an interest in Diane. He sent us to the medical centre in Middlesbrough to see more experts. One gentleman psychologist allowed me to stay as he gave Diane a test. She did well on a few things; others she couldn't understand. He told me he must agree with the other experts. I recall standing up to him and saying, "They can put me in prison yet I will never agree with your diagnosis. God knows my child's future and he will not write her off." Walking away from that building many emotions were sweeping over me but I was aware of the fact that I no longer had the fear of man. From now on I would confront those who were intimidating me. Knowing what the Bible said about fear – that it had torment –

Fear has torment

gave me even more confidence to stand firm and resolute. Praying much about Diane's future, I patiently waited for the letter which would inform us of the classification of our daughter.

My Diane

Chapter 6

The Special School

January of 1971 was just about over. I was very anxious as very soon a letter would be arriving informing us of Diane's classification. That morning the sound of the letter box made me leap out of bed and running downstairs I picked up the letter as if it was a hot coal. My fingers fumbled in haste to open it. Sure enough the experts had made their dreaded pronouncement. My daughter, they had decided, was severely mentally handicapped and would be sent to the Training Centre.

Although I had expected the outcome it was no less shattering to read it in print. Feeling utterly helpless I made myself a cup of coffee and opened my Bible. I read: "If God be for us, who can be against us?" That verse and praying to the Lord quickened

My Diane

my faith once again. At that moment I knew victory was coming, without my striving to intervene.

Nearly three months later another letter arrived. The same experts had changed their minds. Now Diane was to be classified as "educationally subnormal." I felt nothing but derision at this latest move and continued looking after Jack and our three children.

To my amazement, some weeks later, another letter arrived, this time stating that the Committee had decided Diane was 'just a slow learner'. She would be going to a special school of their choice which would be in Diane's interest and provide the best educational future for our daughter. Jack and I were elated at this wonderful news, although there was one drawback. The school was six miles away and she would have to travel on the school bus. We discussed this with our family and came to the conclusion that this was the right decision. I realised that Councillor Stephen Smailes had been fighting for our daughter. He had contacted the Principal School Medical Officer, whose advice had been vital.

The great day arrived for Diane to begin her journey to the special school. As she stepped onto the bus instantly the same feeling of dread that I experienced at the nursing home swept through me. This was the second wrong decision that I had made, the conse-

The special school

quences of which would last for nine years. At the bottom of the final letter it had said "You may appeal against this decision". I know this was where my faith began to waver – just like Peter, the Lord's disciple, who walked on the water when he kept his eyes on Jesus. When he saw the waves and the wind and allowed fear to overtake him, he began to sink. This was how I felt. I was sure this was second best, yet I was in no fit state to oppose the authorities. There was also the thought that Diane would be away all day and I would be able to give more time to Jacqueline and Paul.

At this time the Lord brought a way of escape into my life to take my mind off the hardness of the way. I began to work in the church with the senior citizens. The meeting was given the name 'The Silver Lining'. The work spread out to elderly men and women of different denominations. I had time to visit them and listen to their troubles. I loved the work and the people I came into contact with.

Year one: not too bad

The school bus would drop Diane off near the mainstream school she had previously attended. The first year it wasn't too bad: Diane would come home with spittle running down her face and coat. Pins were

My Diane

stuck in her arms and legs. The children would call her 'Mongol' and 'mental' and she would look bewildered at them.

The real hell on earth were her teenage years. I remember thinking she was old enough to walk the short distance from the bus to our home without my collecting her. It would make her feel independent. One afternoon as I prepared for the late dinner I felt something was wrong. I ran out of the house. Down the main road there are a few side streets and as I reached the second one a large crowd of children was surrounding something. As I drew closer I could see it was Diane. The whole scene reminded me of a pack of baying hounds around a terrified deer. The sight was sickening. They were pushing her from one to the other calling her names and spitting on her. I broke through the ring and scattered them, then promptly went to the school to confront the headmaster who said he would deal with the matter. By now Diane was just a bag of nerves. Her eyes blinked continuously. She couldn't put sentences together; she began to stutter. If I asked her a question she would say, "I can't remember." All we could see now was deterioration.

As I have already mentioned, she particularly feared dogs and she was also terrified of fireworks. I guessed that at some time children had thrown bang-

The special school

ers at her. As I prayed daily for her, God answered my prayers by delivering her from the fear of dogs. A pastor called Ron Smith was so kind and caring. He prayed and fasted for the fear to be lifted. Wonderfully, the fear just left her and after that Diane was able to stroke dogs.

God answered immediately

Another thing I prayed for was regarding the fact that Diane never knew the day or date. God answered immediately. One day she came to me and said, "Mum, it's Saturday, the 14th of June today." I knew another piece of the jigsaw had fallen into place.

Yet for all this she was retreating into herself. I had to speak for her – no one could understand what she was saying – she was unable to communicate. This did not deter me from praying for her. One night after she returned home from school, I ran the bath for her. A while later, as I went to check if she was all right, what a sight met me: Diane's left arm was covered in large purple bruises from her shoulder to her wrist.

"Who's done this?" I asked, thinking she would name an older child. In a small voice she gave me the name of a teacher. Jack and I took her to the police station where photographs were taken of her arm. The police wanted to go to the school to interview this

My Diane

teacher but I said we would deal with it first then come back to them. The next morning I was on that school bus with Diane. My other two children were at school so the whole day was mine.

As we reached the special school I couldn't help thinking, "What if this isn't true?" Going into the headmaster's office and relating the story to him I felt it did sound far fetched. After all, these teachers were trained for this special job. I was feeling a bit of a fool now as I heard the headmaster protesting "No, definitely not, none of my staff would ever do that." Getting up to leave I mentioned the police, telling him that Diane's arm had been photographed.

That same night as we had just finished our late dinner, the doorbell rang. Jack opened the door and who should be standing there but Diane's teacher owning up to the assault on her. More was to come: this same teacher had made Diane stand alone in the car park every play time. "Why?" we asked him. "I just can't take to her," he replied. "She gets on my nerves." Then he said, "I know she is a lonely girl. I've made things worse for her." He broke down, truly repentant. Only that stopped us from going back to the police.

The onslaught continued as we discovered that a boy of fifteen, a bully, had been terrorising her. Once again as I boarded the bus I made a conscious deci-

The special school

sion that this situation had to come to an end. I hid at the back of the bus. Diane had been given instructions not to look round or speak to me. When the bus stopped to let this teenage boy on, I peeped out from the back seat to watch what he might do. Sure enough he swaggered towards my daughter and went for her throat to lift her up out of her seat. To say I was shocked would be an understatement – there was a lady on the bus to look after the children but she didn't seem to be watching them at all. I was out of my seat in a second. "That's it!" I shouted. "You will never do that again!" As the bus stopped in the yard I marched the bully into the headmaster's office. He was genuinely shocked when he realised what had been going on in his school.

I had totally changed

By this time I had totally changed. I now stood up to those who tried to intimidate me. From now on I was determined to make the rules for my daughter who only had one more year to go then she would leave this awful school that had been responsible for reducing her to a nervous wreck. No way would we allow Diane to travel on that school bus. The worst part of it all was that in all this time she had not learned one thing.

My Diane

On top of all this those who loved her could see what effect these traumatic experiences were having on her health. She was losing weight dramatically and her face took on an awful pallor. Very soon things were to come to a head and we would see for ourselves that her body couldn't take much more.

One day, mam, Diane and I went to town to do some shopping. A friend stopped to chat to us. I looked round to see where Diane had gone. She was leaning against a wall. "Are you all right?" I asked her. Without a word she walked towards me. Her lips were bright blue and her face was ashen. She collapsed in my arms. I laid her on the floor. In minutes a crowd had gathered. I heard them saying "This isn't a faint, she's been out too long". This made me afraid. I silently prayed for God to bring her round. A taxi arrived and quickly took us home where I immediately called our doctor out. After examining Diane he said she had experienced a prolonged collapse. I would have to keep her off school for a week.

That night as we helped our daughter to climb the stairs she again collapsed. We had to carry her up to bed, the words of my mother-in-law ringing in my ears. "She'll not see her eighteenth birthday; those children never live very long." Diane was fifteen now. I was determined she would live and not die.

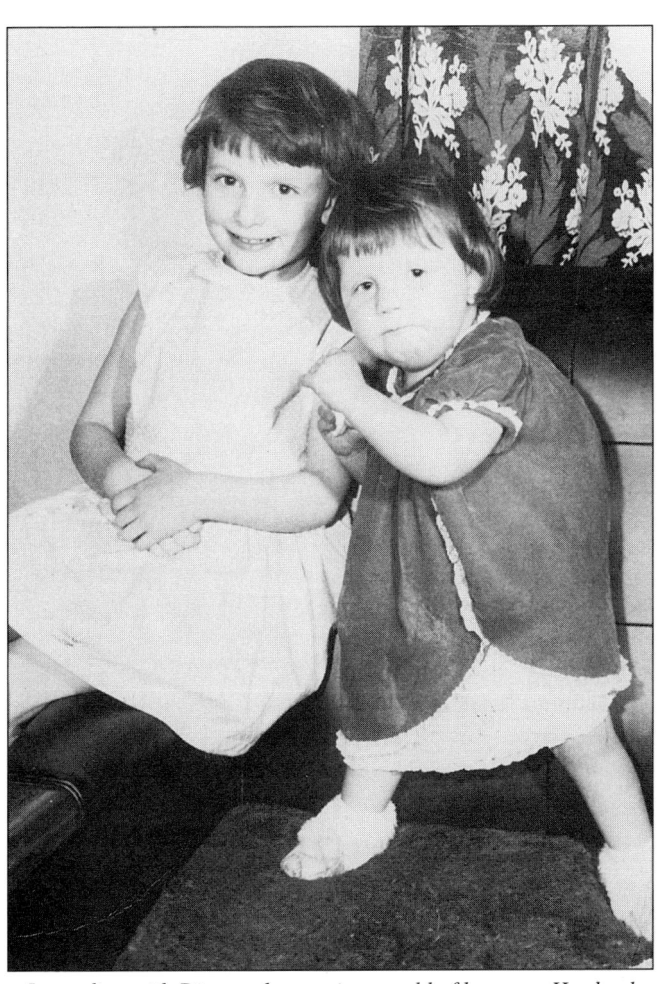

Jacqueline with Diane, who was in a world of her own. Her back was arched and her legs were weak. She fell down after this photo.

The full extent of Diane's brain damage was now evident. At 17 years of age I couldn't leave her alone and had to speak for her.

Diane when she went into town for the first time on her own. Note how her left hand is held in a tight fist, a sympton of cerebral palsy.

*Diane leading the singing at the Silver Liners 25th Anniversary.
The last piece of the jigsaw was at last in its place*

Chapter 7

For this child have I prayed

The next morning I made my way to Diane's bedroom. She was sleeping peacefully, yet I didn't like the colour of her face. It was grey looking and she was breathing rapidly. As I shouted for my husband to get my mother to come and pray with me I was thankful for that small gate connecting our two gardens. It had become a lifeline. My mother was now a widow, dad having died of cancer. My brother, John, and his family had emigrated to Canada and Pam, my sister, had married and was now living in Milton Keynes with her husband, Pastor George Ridley. Only my youngest sister was left at home. Judith and Jacqueline had become qualified hairdressers. Our son, Paul, was twelve-and-a-half and turning into a lovely boy. The one that continued to suffer was Diane.

My Diane

She had no friends, no social life and yet again a further storm was about to break around her.

Hearing mother's footsteps as she came up the stairs brought me comfort as I knew prayer would change things. Mum and I knelt down and called upon the Lord to touch Diane, though this time we felt the heavens were like brass. Looking back it seemed that God had forsaken us. By ten o'clock in the evening her condition had deteriorated. We had no other choice but to phone the emergency doctor and within fifteen minutes he was at our front door. We showed him into Diane's room and waited anxiously for his diagnosis. After seeing Diane he took us aside and said, "Your daughter has pneumonia and fluid on the lungs. She is also very anaemic." I don't know to this day how she escaped from being hospitalised. Maybe the Lord knew I could not take any more.

Diane was ill for six weeks. In that time she changed dramatically. Up until then she had been well-made with a round, plumpish face. Now all the weight dropped off her, making her face look gaunt. Looking back, I vividly remember persistently praying. The story of Hannah, the mother of Samuel the prophet, inspired me. When God answered her prayer she said "For this child I have prayed," (1 Samuel ch1 v 27).

I wept like Hannah, pouring out my soul to God, visualising Diane completely whole, even though she

For this child have I prayed

was becoming worse. This is the very essence of faith, taking our eyes off what surrounds us and looking to God who rewards those who diligently seek him.

Not long afterwards I recall sitting down with my husband and discussing the possibility of moving again. Jack laughed, saying that we were like gypsies and that it would be our fourth move. However, he would agree to it if we could find a nice bungalow.

A new beginning

Everything began to move so quickly. My brother, John, and family, returned home from Canada. We made a decision to leave the church in Stockton and attend the New Life Pentecostal Church in Billingham. The minister was Cliff Henderson. Jack and I found a lovely bungalow situated about a mile away. We were very happy when we found out there were no children in the road. I believed again that it would be a new beginning.

Moving out of the crescent and into the bungalow kept me sane. The thought that Diane would be leaving that awful special school when she turned sixteen, filled me with joy. By this time my next-door neighbour was speaking to me. She even came to church with us but still there was a huge relief when once again we set off for our new home.

My Diane

This time it was different. Our neighbour had coffee and biscuits waiting for us. Everyone treated us with respect and for once, as a family, we felt at peace with our surroundings. Jack and I talked late into the night. We both felt that this was the turning point for Diane. A small minibus was sent to pick her up outside our home and take her to school. There were to be no more incidents of bullying. The torment was over and the months passed quickly to 25th July, Diane's sixteenth birthday. We celebrated not only her birthday but the fact that she would never have to go back to school again.

By now Jacqueline was working for a young man called Richard Trent. Soon, she had me working part-time in his hair salon. One day Diane came in with me and Richard kindly let her help by taking rollers out of the clients' hair. I recall perming a lady's hair when she suddenly caught hold of my hand saying, "Look at that poor girl. Isn't it a terrible shame." As I turned round and saw Diane I knew this was the girl she was talking about. With a sweet smile I replied "Do you mean my daughter? Oh, she's fine. There's nothing wrong with her." At that precise moment I felt a dread that again another trial was heading our way. It wouldn't come from my neighbours, they were lovely; our new home was perfect; it couldn't come from the school – Diane had left. "Where then?" I

For this child have I prayed

asked myself. The answer soon came.

Complete strangers were to bring hell into our short-lived peaceful lives. One morning Diane and I got on a bus to go to town. I walked to the back of the bus and sat down. Diane was slowly trying to join me. Four young women on the bus looked up and down at my daughter then broke into very loud laughter at Diane's expense. For two long years this continued. She couldn't walk down the town or catch a bus without teenagers shouting abuse and laughing at her scornfully.

"Lord, show me what others see."

I cried, "Lord Jesus, show me what others are seeing when they stare at my daughter." That afternoon I had reason to visit Marks & Spencers. Going through the doors into the store, a large, full-length mirror was right in front of me. Diane, who was following me, came into view. My prayer was answered. Shock was registered on my face as I saw in that mirror the state she was in. Her countenance was like a mask. Her eyes were sunken with black rings round them; her face seemed to be dragged down on the left side. She looked vacant and remote.

I was convinced much more prayer was needed; I would never let go of the promises of God. For this

My Diane

child, I told myself, I would keep on praying. My faith was quickened; prayer became bold and powerful. Never would I listen to the negative opinions of others. Even Christians would say, "Well, sometimes it's the will of God," or "Diane is your cross, you will just have to bear it." This made me understand why Jesus had told the crowd of people to leave the room while he performed the miraculous healing of Jairus' daughter, because he knew unbelief was present.

The promises of God contradicted everything the critics were telling me. The Bible says: "Without faith it is impossible to please God." Now he was encouraging me to walk by faith. This trial would not crush me, but refine me; it would change and transform me in preparation for service. Looking back over the years everything seems much clearer. Out of ashes and seeming defeat, the Lord had plans for my life; shortly these plans would unfold and I would be led into a ministry that was exciting and fulfilling. My calling would be confirmed time after time.

Chapter 8

God's way of escape

How many parents have cried out in anguish, "If only I could run away!" I would say to myself, "Oh, if I had the wings of a dove then I would fly away." My life now needed a diversion. I yearned for the wings of an eagle that would take me high and wide and give me a greater perspective on life. How I thank God that, like a mother eagle who swoops down to save its young ones from being dashed to pieces, so my heavenly Father gave me a way of escape so that I could bear the burden which was threatening to crush me. I needed to escape from thoughtless and insensitive words from Christians. Diane was being ignored and treated as invisible. She had no friends outside the Church and none within it. It was becoming very

My Diane

hard for me to keep a sweet spirit.

God's leading for us as a family took us to the New Life Pentecostal Church at Billingham, where I was asked by Pastor Cliff Henderson to start the Silver Liners ministry for senior citizens. The congregation was small in number, between twelve and twenty-four gathered week by week, but as we fervently prayed for increase we began to see steady growth.

The numbers in the Silver Liners for a few years remained at just twelve members, yet we were reaching out to nursing homes, sheltered accommodation, plus over-sixties clubs. Looking back to those wonderful opportunities to share the gospel I recall two remarkable experiences where we could see the Lord was plainly working.

One of those experiences was a gentleman called Ernie who lived in Stockton. I was a regular visitor to his home as I used to do his wife's hair. I've never seen such a devoted couple. They had no family, but this didn't seem to bother them. I talked to his wife about salvation and she became a Christian. Ernie, on the other hand, wasn't sure if there was a Creator.

One day his wife was rushed to hospital where she died. Ernie was inconsolable. I remember standing with him beside the garden gate as he cried out, "There is no God," with tears streaming down his face.

God's way of escape

He called after me: "Don't send any pastors or church members here. I don't want to see anyone." My heart was heavy as I returned home because I knew he was rejecting the only one that could give him eternal life and a purpose to go on.

One year later his house went up for sale. I just thought, "That's it – he's died." Some time later a desire to visit a nursing home in Fairfield seemed to be always coming into my mind. I shared this with Pastor Cliff and we subsequently arranged for a meeting to be held there. Included in my programme for the visit was to be the testimony of one of the Silver Liners – a man in his eighties. Pastor Bill Strike would follow this with a short preaching of the Word.

"Please stay and listen"

Arriving at the gates of the home a thought passed through my mind: "Would I know any of the residents?" As we walked into the large room the first face I saw was Ernie's. When he saw me he got up to leave. "Please stay and listen for a while," I pleaded with him. As he took his seat again, the elderly Christian gentleman began his testimony: "I had a lovely wife whom I loved with all my heart. On her deathbed she said to me: 'When I die I know where I'm going but I don't know where you're going because

My Diane

you don't believe in God. All these years we have been together yet we will spend eternity parted.'" He went on to say how he had knelt at the foot of the cross and repented. Following on from this the Word was faithfully proclaimed.

I looked over at Ernie who was now weeping, only this time they were tears of repentance as he accepted the Lord Jesus as his Saviour. We booked a further visit and on our return we were told Ernie had died. God in His mercy and patience had waited for him to get right and turn from his unbelief, then He took him home.

Looking back to the times when we held meetings in the sheltered homes, one lady in particular I will never forget. She had a small cancerous growth on her lip. As we took the meetings the gospel songs thrilled her. She was very attentive to the word of God but in time, because of increasing numbers in the Silver Liners, we stopped going out to some of the venues.

It was quite some time before I saw her again. A lady phoned me asking if I would visit her as the cancer had spread rapidly. Stepping into her little flat, the sight that met me was heartbreaking. I said "You need the Lord". Her answer took me by surprise, "I know I do," she replied. If she had ranted and raved, demanding to know why He had allowed this to happen to her, I could have understood, yet in perfect

God's way of escape

peace she called upon the Lord.

Until her death we went and sang all the gospel songs to her. I can picture her now, conducting the singers – the bravest woman I have ever had the privilege to know. The family asked me to sing The Old Rugged Cross at her funeral.

Diane's eighteenth birthday

Thus, for a time, my mind was taken off Diane. I wasn't so anxious when she kept on collapsing. My eyes were on God. He wanted me to continue to trust Him regardless of the circumstances. I would not believe that God had finished with my daughter. Her eighteenth birthday was celebrated with our Christian friends at New Life Church, then once again Jack and I decided to make one final move. The reason for this was that the bungalow was now far too small. Jacqueline was courting, Paul had many friends and when the family came to visit the lounge could not accommodate them all.

We were sorry to leave that road for we had found such peace and happiness in it. Jack didn't have to engage an estate agent – word of mouth brought a buyer. Within months we were preparing for our fifth and final move.

Our decision was to purchase a three-bedroomed

My Diane

semi-detached house again. Bungalows were out of the question now. The day we moved in I couldn't help but wonder what the house and area would be like to live in, so it was with some relief I found the neighbours very friendly. Also, once again, the vendor had left everything spotless.

Now and again little answers to my prayers came to uplift me. Diane met up with a girl who used to attend the special school. Once a week they would have a meal together. Her name was Marie and Diane looked forward to seeing her.

I started a part-time job in a nursing home as a carer, looking after people suffering from Alzheimer's disease. Even that was in God's plans for my life. Diane was allowed to help me – the doctor called it 'therapeutic' – but after a year it became too much for her and she began to collapse again even more frequently than before. On several occasions, after she'd had a bath, I would find her on the floor.

My experience of looking after patients with Alzheimer's was to prove invaluable, for my father-in-law, after the death of his wife and coming to live with us, suffered from this disease.

In my heart I felt the Lord was saying, "Barbara, you often declare you love older people. Now show me. I've placed him in your home for you to show him My love and care." He lived with us four years

God's way of escape

and I know it was God who gave me the strength, patience and love to cope.

Vivid memories

There are lots of vivid memories whirling around in my mind and yet there were also dormant periods when nothing seemed to be happening. I was aware, however, that spiritually I was growing. My prayer would be: "Lord, take Diane forward again," which, to my delight, He did. Her face started to lose that vacant look. Her eyes began to show life. When she was bridesmaid at her sister's wedding, I felt so proud of her. Jacqueline and Diane looked beautiful on the photographs. On her twenty-first birthday Diane had to give a speech and though she had to be prompted even for the shortest sentence, I was still seeing more progress.

For a time our lives seemed to be ambling along without too much stress and strain until one evening. We had just returned home from church when Diane suddenly burst into floods of tears: "Mum, I have no friends in that church." That night I heard her crying in bed. I knew then she understood what was going on around her; that she longed for the young people to say more than just, "Hello, Diane." Yet she couldn't communicate with them and frustration was building

My Diane

up inside of her. She was so unhappy and this affected me. I knew a nervous breakdown would be next for Diane or myself if things didn't change. Just one week later she made her own decision. "Mum," she said, "I want to go to the Ragworth Fellowship with Uncle John and Jan."

Thankfully, that request had come at just the right time because I felt I couldn't go on much longer. The sorrow and anguish of those long, difficult years was taking its toll on my health. It culminated in two days and nights of unrelenting weeping from the very depth of my being. My eyes became so swollen I had to wear sunglasses to hide them. I knew it was vital for Diane and me to both have a break from each other. It would be beneficial for both of us. A sense of relief swept over me as God's peace came back into my heart. A way of escape had again been given to me.

Diane settled in quickly at her new church. Our neighbours, Ian and Irene Maclean, kindly took her in their car every week. The pressure was now lessening. I drummed it into Diane that she hadn't to rely on the young people for friendship. She was now a woman and those childhood to teenage years which ought to have been full of fun, love and laughter – so-called normality – had been denied her. Poignantly, Diane understood this.

Approximately five years ago my daughter,

God's way of escape

Jacqueline and I bought the lease of a hairdressing salon which would expire after a few years. Diane would be able to do a few simple jobs and this would stimulate her mind. The first week of being in the salon brought a new confidence to her. One day a major breakthrough gave me another piece of the jigsaw. Diane had never been able to catch a normal bus on her own – she didn't know the names of any of the shops. But that day she just came out with the statement that she wanted to go to the town by herself to buy a couple of jumpers. "I'll also have some lunch," she concluded. Jacqueline and I were shocked but I said, "All right, but be back for three o'clock." All afternoon we were on edge. At five-to-three there was no sign of her. We began to panic, thinking she wouldn't find her way back to the salon. But at three o'clock the door opened and in she walked! She told us exactly where she had been and what she had done. At last God had brought her out of that horrible darkness. He had released her memory and set her free.

Gaining more confidence

Every day she gained more confidence and listening to the ladies laughing and joking with each other seemed to bring her out of her shyness. The clients loved her and she loved them Soon we were to

My Diane

leave the salon but they said they would never forget us. That Christmas I put on a running buffet every day for a week. Backing tracks, microphone and karaoke were installed. Carols and gospel music were played. We sang those beautiful songs to a captive audience. They loved every minute of it, not wanting to go home.

As I reminisce about the past, some things just seem to make sense now, whereas years ago it seemed so unfair. Diane was the reason I left the first hairdressing business. Then I had come out with losses. This time I had come out victorious – not with money, but with people whom I had won for Christ. They still come to church with me to this day. The greatest gain from this business was Diane's miracle. It played a part in her recovery – God has evened the score.

When Diane was nearly thirty years old I felt the Lord speaking to me about coming back to my home church at Stockton. I tried to push it to the back of my mind as I was happy at Billingham but when I was praying at the front of the church I felt God was saying it was time to go back. In obedience I did what He was asking of me. After six months His plans were to be revealed: the leader of the Silver Liners there was planning to retire. Would I be willing to become the leader?

Peace filled my mind as I accepted the proposal.

God's way of escape

Time was to demonstrate that this was of the Lord. A team of ladies formed a gospel group with myself, and Diane joined us. She has a sweet voice and, funnily enough, she sings a duet with Moira, who is amazed at the transforming work of God.

My Diane

Chapter 9

The right diagnosis

The 12th May 1997 was the most incredible day of my life – and to think that I nearly didn't keep the appointment! The DHSS had written to ask that I take Diane to be examined by their own independent doctor. As Jack and I discussed taking her by car to the large building which was quite a long journey, I felt less than enthusiastic when I thought of the experts talking about my daughter and then proceeding to talk over her head as if she wasn't in the room. In my own mind I questioned whether or not this doctor would be any different.

Jack booked a day's holiday so that he could be with us to hear the latest opinion about our daughter. While Diane and I entered the building my husband sat in the car reading the paper. At reception we filled

My Diane

in a form before being ushered into a fairly large office where a kindly looking doctor welcomed us. As he closed the door I couldn't help thinking he must be near to retirement.

As we sat there he said, "I won't talk to Diane, it will be quicker just talking to you, Mrs Ryder."

"Typical," I thought. "I was right. He is just the same as all the others who wrote her off as having no IQ. She's just a cabbage to them."

In fact his eyes never looked at her at all. Pen in hand he proceeded to fire questions at me. In about ten minutes most of Diane's life had been recorded again. Then suddenly I felt a rush of adrenaline. "This is going down the same road again," I told myself. "God help me find some answers," What happened next no one could have prepared me for. I was in shock as my two questions to this doctor brought answers that overwhelmed me. Diane had now taken all of his attention. Staring into her face he began talking, and I heard him mention the words 'stroke', 'the palsy', 'her speech'. I knew nothing about palsy but in my heart there was a strong feeling that this was the right diagnosis. Sitting there every emotion swept over me. Joy, happiness, gratitude – strangely enough, bitterness was far from my thoughts.

Thanking the doctor for his kindness, Diane and I rose up to leave. He said, "Your daughter's recovery

The right diagnosis

is amazing." My parting words were: "Yes, and it's all down to prayer." He nodded at me in agreement.

Walking out through the entrance I turned to take a final look at the building when something stirred in my memory. As I stood outside the Medical Centre, the years rolled away. I remembered bringing Diane to this very building when she was just seven. The experts – the psychologists and doctors – had written her off. Now here she was aged thirty-three standing next to me and the Lord God had other plans for her life. The final piece of the jigsaw was now in place. Tears started to run down my face. This time they were tears of joy. Diane had been released from her walking coma. Putting my arms around her we walked to the car to share the wonderful news with her father.

"What did the doctor say?"

Jack spoke first. "Well, what did the doctor say?" As I told him the doctor's diagnosis he looked shaken. "You mean to say we have brought up a daughter who's been physically handicapped, not mentally handicapped and not one expert has been able to see it till now?" He was livid. On the journey home I knew exactly what my next step would be. I wanted this confirming. Questions needed to be answered – of which I had plenty.

My Diane

The following day the wheels were set in motion. I phoned the palsy line. How ironic that the only collecting I had ever been asked to do in our crescent was for Scope, formerly known as the Spastic Society. Cerebral palsy had replaced the word 'spastic' and I was still ignorant as to what it was, yet I knew Jesus had healed many with the palsy when he was on earth. The Bible tells of these miracles.

As the lady returned my call she was most helpful. Diane's past symptoms pointed to hemiplegia which had paralysed her down the left side leaving her with learning difficulties. Replacing the telephone and then making a coffee I sat down to thank God for his mercy and goodness. To all intents and purposes my daughter should have been confined to a wheelchair. Everything became clear as my mind went back to the time she lay on the floor moaning, hands and feet moving in agony. What we had witnessed were the involuntary muscle spasms that a child with cerebral palsy apparently suffers. Mercifully, God had taken those away and her back, which had been very arched, He had straightened. Now I began to understand the reason for all the other symptoms: her legs, which seemed as if they had no muscles in them; her left arm, which she could hardly use and her hand so weak that even to hold a fork was an effort; her mouth, droopy at one side, but when she cried it would sag

The right diagnosis

right down. The worst effect of the palsy had been Diane's speech – her vocal chords had been paralysed. Communication had been virtually impossible for many years. The sad part was that she had known a lot of what was going on yet withdrew into herself, letting me talk for her until it had become second nature.

I made an appointment to see our new doctor. He had never met Diane so wouldn't know anything of her medical history. I felt very nervous when the morning arrived in which I would once again have to recount Diane's life and re-open old wounds.

"What time is it, Diane?"

As we walked into his office I knew at last this doctor would listen and be prepared to get something done. His kind face, his relaxed manner, put Diane and me at ease. Going over the story of my daughter's life he kept glancing at her. When I had finished he said, "She knows what we are saying?"

"Yes" I replied, "she knows everything we are saying."

"What time is it, Diane?" the doctor asked her.

"Ten o'clock" she replied.

We carried on talking then he repeated the same question.

My Diane

"It's twenty-past ten now," Diane answered.

Smiling at us he told me Diane would have to be examined by a neurologist, though he could see it had been cerebral palsy, recognising it from her mouth. Leaving the surgery, then getting into the car to drive home, my thoughts were so mixed up. Diane seemed very nervous. Her eyelids were blinking rapidly. I felt like leaving things alone. Were we stirring up a hornet's nest?

Once we arrived home and I discussed things with the family I went a step further, saying a brain scan should be considered. To my relief we only had to wait about two months before we could see the consultant. Sitting in the department of neurology I couldn't help but notice how beautiful Diane looked. Her eyes were full of life. As for her listening to every detail of her life being scrutinised again, I wondered what she was thinking. She certainly looked calm.

The nurse beckoned us into the large office where once again my daughter's life from birth to adult life was recounted. I had difficulty keeping back the tears. The doctor gave Diane some tests. I noticed he was observing her left hand. He nodded. "Yes, it's been cerebral palsy. How do you account for her remarkable recovery?"

"Every day I've prayed for her and wouldn't let go of God," I replied.

The right diagnosis

"Well, it has worked" the neurologist said.

Half expecting him to refuse, I asked if Diane could have a brain scan. "Yes," he said "leave that to me. It will be arranged and an appointment will be sent to you."

How I thanked God deep inside me for his goodness. I knew the results of the scan would be favourable. My fear was Diane's reaction when she had to go into the machine. The many tales of adults not being able to cope with the sensation of being confined in a very small space troubled me. Would she panic and the brain scan have to be postponed?

My fears were groundless, for on the day of this important hospital visit Diane just didn't seem to care, even though she knew what to expect. As we chatted in the waiting room, the two young men who were also going to have scans looked scared. When Diane's turn came she went in smiling and returned laughing. "It was nothing, mum," she told me. "I wasn't frightened at all. All I can remember was being churned up and as tense as a board."

"Why didn't I trust you more?"

"Lord," I cried, "Why didn't I trust you more? She hadn't needed to be sedated – you made her calm. Thank you, God."

My Diane

All we needed now was patience to wait for the results. On the morning of my birthday, 25 September, as I collected the many cards from the hall I remarked to Diane how it seemed that the older one got the more cards one seemed to receive. Eagerly opening them one by one, I found to my surprise one letter was from the hospital. As I read out aloud its contents I realised that this just had to be the best birthday present ever. The scan had shown Diane's brain to have no abnormalities; no scars were on the brain. Her reading was clear.

We were ecstatic. This was what we had expected and hoped for, and even more confirmation was around the corner indicating that the Lord was sweeping away every dark veil that had been like a shroud keeping the truth hidden from view. My God was now showing me his power in a greater way. Every prayer was being answered. All the people from twenty-six years ago were being placed in my pathway. I didn't have to seek them out – it was incredible.

The first encounter was the retired headmaster, Bob Jones. We met up again at his mother's funeral. Speaking to him later I asked him what his assessment of Diane had been all those years ago. Without any hesitation he said: "Cerebral palsy. Of course she should have been in a wheelchair. God's been good."

"How could you have known that?" I asked him.

The right diagnosis

"Because I was headmaster at a school for children with the same disability. They were spastic."

My face lit up at this further confirmation of the truth. How I longed to meet again the young teacher who had taught Diane at the mainstream school. She would be about forty-eight now. Would I recognise her? She may have changed so much, or more probably moved out of the area.

My wish had been granted

The next week on a busy market day, as I was strolling past the various stalls, my eyes scanning the crowds, my heart leapt. Walking towards me was Diane's teacher. My wish had been granted. As I made myself known to her she enquired about Diane, saying she hadn't forgotten her. As we reminisced about the past, I reminded her of the day she told me that Diane, at only six years old, could identify over one hundred words by just pointing to the word.

"I left shortly after Diane for a new post" she said.

"What was that?" I enquired.

"Oh, a school for physically handicapped children. They have cerebral palsy."

I shook my head in disbelief. If only we had known the right diagnosis all those years ago this lovely teacher would still have been teaching Diane in her

My Diane

school for special children with spastic hemiplegia etc., right up to the date of her leaving school. "Never mind, that's all in the past," I told myself.

As I said goodbye to that teacher I wondered who else from the past would cross my pathway. A few weeks later a pleasant surprise was awaiting me. Some of my friends from the Silver Liners were helping me with a cake stall. We needed funds to buy a minibus. Other stalls for charity were around us and who should be next to us but Councillor Stephen Smailes. After meeting Diane again I'm sure he was delighted that his fight for her had proved to be right and just.

In quick succession we were bumping into young married women who had known Diane as a child. It was a tonic to me as I watched their faces as I told them the truth about her. An invitation came for us to go to the wedding of a young man who also knew Diane. His family were amazed when they saw her. Their faces said it all: "Can this be the girl who couldn't speak, the one who children laughed to scorn?"

My heart missed a beat when the groom hugged Diane and whispered, "You look beautiful today." These were words I thought I would never hear from people. We were only used to words that wounded but such as these would heal and encourage.

"Shall we have a day out by the seaside?" I asked

The right diagnosis

my friends. The trip ended at Redcar where shops were visited in quick succession then, feeling peckish we ended up in a charming cafe on the way to Marske. During the meal a middle-aged couple brought in a young man who was confined to a wheelchair. I didn't take much notice of him at first until he began to speak. He sounded just like Diane when she was younger. As I looked at his left hand it was held in a position that she used to hold. His back was arched and he was hanging over the side of the chair, just like Diane did as a little girl. At that precise moment I knew that if God had not healed her, my daughter would have been exactly like this young man, whom I now recognised as having cerebral palsy. Some mother's son: my heart went out to him and to his carers – those special people – who are given qualities that are to be greatly admired. May God bless them all.

My Diane

Chapter 10

From a mother to a mother

Life is full of mysteries. The unexplained will always baffle and frustrate mankind, especially the supernatural. We always desire to see before we will believe. I find it incredible that the majority of us take ourselves for granted, not accepting the simple truth of God's word that, "we are fearfully and wonderfully made," (Psalm 139:14). Yet so many still refuse to acknowledge God as Creator. Their minds are tormented with questions and unbelief, rejecting any light from the written word. They prefer their equilibrium to be undisturbed. "Keep out," is what they say to God when he stands at the door and knocks.

Most people have an inner sanctum, a place within their hearts or minds where memories are stored away, with the ability to recall events from the past when-

My Diane

ever they wish, usually to cheer or amuse. At times, thoughts will come, unbidden, into their minds to disturb or provoke. Those memories that cause distress tend to be kept in that inner room where hurt and unforgiveness are their companions.

I had such a place in my mind that had been locked for thirty-three years. A book was in there longing to be released – the smallest detail, exact conversations, vivid pictures pouring out of my mind as if on film. Many tears have been shed again as old wounds have re-opened and forgiveness has come to many of those people who, for many years, caused me and my family so much pain. Yet these scars must be completely erased. Lying on a psychiatrist's couch, or being counselled may seem the right choice for many people. As for me I am permitting the Lord to enter and begin the inner healing, emptying every memory that seeks to chain me; cleansing the chamber, permeating it with his love and presence, removing all the scars – as he did for Diane.

Our lives have been interwoven all these years yet she is not loved any more than her siblings. The stark fact is that Diane has always needed me and, as one given charge of a special child, I have been like a mother hen, sheltering her. She is *my* Diane. My life has been enriched by having her as my daughter. I have learned patience. I now have the ability to be

From a mother to a mother

moved with compassion and understanding, especially for those carers who look after the sick and disabled, both young and old. Most of all I can empathise with every mother who has had those words spoken to her by the professionals in white coats: "I am afraid your child is disabled." The shock and grief that follows the diagnosis progresses into many strong emotions until, finally, acceptance is the norm.

Nothing is too hard for God

Maybe if I had just accepted what I was fully aware of – that Diane was different from Jacqueline and Paul – life would have been a lot easier. Yet it was never in my mind to be defeated. Nothing is too hard for God, including the mind. What is brain damage to him?

There are ten mothers that I know who have a child who is physically handicapped. What shines out of these wonderful carers is their love and devotion. I salute you all. I can identify with what you are going through. Perhaps the pouring out of my thoughts will be beneficial to you as you realise that the long waiting periods in Diane's life were not God's denials. On the contrary, my faith was being increased as I was being stretched to lay hold of God in persistent prayer.

Have you ever considered what the outcome might

My Diane

have been if Abraham had continued to intercede for the inhabitants of Sodom and Gomorrah? God said, "I will not destroy the city for the sake of ten," then Abraham left off speaking (Genesis 18:32 AV). He seemed reluctant to ask any more.

Many times we give up on God's promises before they have time to be fulfilled in our lives. Faith and patience go hand in hand in the Bible and the saints of old were exercised by them. The fact is they are examples to us of great perseverance in spite of the difficulties and suffering.

Even the strongest person might break if kept too long under unrelieved tension. I know by experience that my heavenly Father will not allow his children who trust in him to be crushed by burdens too heavy to bear. When we take his yoke upon us the way becomes easier and bearable. God always responds to the broken-hearted.

There are some things in life that amaze me. One of these is that of being foster parents. Their role of rearing a child that is not their own, loving and protecting it, is incredible to me. When that child has disabilities it is a special foster mother that is needed.

My Christian friend, Helen, took on such a role fourteen years ago, taking Michael into her home, despite being aware of his disabilities. With her husband and their children, they took on this challenge

From a mother to a mother

which demanded total dedication and love for this boy.

Helen has kindly given me her contribution to this chapter. She shares with us how she now understands what carers of disabled children go through because of ignorance from some people who shun any child who is handicapped:

Foster parents

When we first met Michael, he was 12 years old, very small and thin for his age with beautiful blue eyes and fair hair. You couldn't tell by looking at Michael that he had severe learning difficulties. We became his foster parents, and so began a new life where we learned what it means to have a child who isn't like other children.

One of Michael's habits when he first came to live with us was what we call 'twinkling' (waggling his fingers whilst holding his hand quite close to his face and staring at his fingers with great concentration). One day, not long after he came to live with us, we took Michael to town and went to look around Woolworth's. I was holding his hand firmly because he would run off and had no sense of danger and also because the shop was full of lovely things which would attract Michael's attention and which he would pick up. I felt someone watching me and when I turned

My Diane

round a lady was staring at us. I realised she had a little girl, aged about three, who was standing a few feet away and watching entranced as Michael 'twinkled' away with his fingers. Michael and I were standing between the little girl and her mother. I don't know what I imagined, but I certainly didn't expect the reaction this lady had. She never spoke to Michael or to me, but told her little girl to, "Come along, darling, come this way," and signalled with her hand to show she wanted the little girl to go around Michael giving him a very wide berth. I was so amazed and her reaction was so unexpected that I couldn't think of anything to say. I felt hurt for Michael but horrified that anyone, especially another mother, could behave as this lady did. In effect, she was teaching her child that Michael, because he was different, was someone to be feared and avoided at all costs. I wished I had thought quickly enough to say to that mother that we don't have a so-called 'normal' child because we deserve it, any more that we have a child who is disabled in any way, whether physically or mentally, because we have done something wrong. It can happen to any one of us.

Sharing the last fourteen years with Michael has made our lives very different. We've had some difficult times and sometimes felt very aware of the restrictions that caring for Michael has put on our own, and on our children's lives. However, knowing Michael has brought tears, joy and a lot of laughter into all of our lives and we've learned so much about living in Michael's world that we would never have known. He taught us to see the person behind the 'handicap'.

"Are you bitter?"

People often ask me, "Are you bitter that it's taken thirty-three years to get the correct diagnosis for Diane?" I always reply, "No", because I am the better for it. God has done a work in me as well as my daughter. It's the Lord who has done this miracle. All the glory and thanks go to him. No medical person, speech therapist, or physiotherapist can take any credit for bringing Diane on because none of these professionals ever gave her any treatment. She was not known to them. I am so glad God didn't pass her by and that he gave me my heart's desire – to be able to communicate with my daughter – which is marvellous. Our lives are enriched through having a special child. I can look back on it all now and say, "Forgetting those things that are behind and looking to a bright tomorrow, where faith in God takes us forward." I am leaving negative attitudes way back and taking hold of the promises of God.

My Diane

Mothers, when you despair because your child has learning difficulties, just remember some other traits they are devoid of: jealousy, envy, pride, gossip, anger and hatred. My Diane has never displayed any of these baser characteristics. I recall a lady telling me that her six-year-old Down's syndrome boy had to be taught to do naughty things. She said he was such a well-behaved child this helped her to cope.

I thank God for our three grandchildren, Joel, Niall and Leah. They are all strong and healthy. I pray that each will have an understanding of anyone young or old who has any disability and realise, that "there, but for the grace of God, go I."

Chapter 11
Not a cross, a blessing

The old years over, another year ahead of us. "Don't look back!" is my heart's cry, yet my mind tells me to take just one final look. I find the inevitable happening. I am recalling Diane's birth, reliving the midwives rushing away with my silent, motionless baby. I know now that both the brain damage, due to a lack of oxygen, and the damage to her nose, were incurred during the birth. A retired midwife has now explained some of the reasons for this happening.

The long delay in being able to speak, the difficulty of finding a way to communicate, must have been so frustrating for Diane, especially when people asked me what she was saying. I had to be her voice –

My Diane

at the doctor's, the dentist's, the hospital, for phone calls. How often I wondered what she was thinking – only God knew.

Thought and language are so closely intermingled. The paralysis prevented any intelligence being vocalised which resulted in much misunderstanding towards Diane. I am now fully aware of what people thought of her. One lady looked me in the eyes and said "Oh, she never had anything in her brain, did she?" The pain I felt at that moment was so intense that I couldn't speak, yet my innermost thoughts were of pity for this person who had what Diane had not – she had the power of speech, but her tongue was a two-edged sword.

My next-door neighbour has told me that when we moved in to our house Diane would peep through the net curtains longingly, watching her three teenage girls playing. They thought she was an old lady with her stark, white face. Now these girls are married with children of their own, they have seen the marvellous transformation and know that Diane can match them in looks and style now.

There are also the sceptics who are not willing to attribute this wonderful miracle to the Lord. They remark: "Isn't nature good at righting itself?" or, "Well she wasn't that bad, just a little slow."

Negative words have lost their effect on me. I have

Not a cross, a blessing

also found out something marvellous. The tears and pain have gone. As I recall events I can smile now as I remember a young mother giving me a serious lecture: "God has sent you your child as a cross and you will have to carry that cross." What a statement! What a distortion of the Lord's words!

A cross is an instrument of torture and severe suffering for the victim, ending in death. In his plan of salvation, God allowed his son, Jesus, to carry his cross and then, like a lamb, submit himself to its savagery at Calvary. To think that I could accept that God wanted me to bear a cross makes me recoil in horror. The cross which I am asked to take up daily is recorded in Luke 9:23, where Jesus says that those who would follow him must take up their cross. In other words, we must die to self, crucifying the lusts and affections we have and identify ourselves with Christ, not being afraid of reproach and scorn because we are Christians. This cross I gladly bear; it is my cross.

Enriched by Diane

My family and I can categorically say Diane has been a blessing and our lives have been enriched by her. My own character has certainly been formed through having a special child. The troubles and disappointments have produced in me patience, strength

My Diane

and resilience. Opposition from those who delighted to intimidate only served to create a boldness and a trust in a God of justice. I no longer feared the opinions of others. The greatest gain for me was a compassion for others and an ever-increasing faith as I was called upon to exercise it, knowing from experience that what seemed a stumbling block one moment, would be cleared away further down the road.

Yes, the Lord has done great things for Diane and my heart is full of gratitude and praise for healing, both inside and out. I don't want to hang around any longer with the past. This is now a new year, a new beginning. What is past is past. I am looking ahead. Time flies and spring will soon be here with its usual throwing out of useless clutter. I will empty cupboards, wardrobes and cases to see what must go.

Yet what will be brought out but not thrown away will be those precious possessions that mean so much to me. From the large box where they are lovingly stored will come photographs of all three children, of when they were babies and then at school. There will be letters and doctors' reports. Most mothers have these treasures which are irreplaceable if lost.

I get such delight when, with my family, I watch the video of Diane's 21st birthday party and hear Pastor Cliff Henderson praying to God to complete the

Not a cross, a blessing

work he has begun in our daughter. All those years later I am able to phone Cliff and tell him that the work is complete.

"It's time to write that book now, Barbara", he said when I gave him the news. That was the confirmation I needed, for God had already put it in my heart to begin writing. Pastor Cliff is a great encourager; a minister always there for us; a man we highly esteem in the Lord.

I thank God for Mrs Christine Thwaites, who gave of her time to help Diane with reading and writing. I realise the best progress has come through daily reading of her Bible, which was kindly given to her by Ron, one of our silver liners. Also, prayer has become important to her.

"Lord, quicken my mind."

I was amazed one morning when she prayed, "Lord, quicken my mind. I am not going to be slow for I can do all things through Christ, who strengthens me." She is praying for herself now. God will not deny any good thing to those who walk uprightly.

What I have seen tells me she is continuing to develop in her thinking and understanding. Every day brings some new delight to my heart because I am expecting to see it. At Christmas people sent her cards.

My Diane

One morning Diane showed me the ones with Father Christmas on the front. "Mum," she said, "why do people send me cards like this when I am an adult?"

I just smiled to myself, thinking, "Welcome to our world, daughter." This was the first of many "Why, mums?" Diane never ever asked questions in the past. She never asked us to buy her anything for Christmas or birthdays. Now she is taking a great interest in her bedroom, asking for a new carpet and curtains! She keeps her room spotless. I know it can only get better for I shall continue to pray the gifts and talents that God has placed within her will surface, as I pray that for my other two children. Even though they are in their thirties and think they don't need a mother's prayers, they are still the fruit of my womb and I know God will bless them, drawing them to himself.

Jack and I may have made mistakes when bringing up our three children but I know for sure God's way. The right way to live in his sight has been spoken of many times in our home. Our children are now responsible for their own actions and their own children will remind them of what they were like as teenagers. Life is like a circle and keeps going round. One thing we can't stop is age. One day they will be where we are now. Our grandchildren delight our hearts and we are content to spend time at home most of the week, not seeking after clubs, pubs and enter-

Not a cross, a blessing

tainment. We have done all that, and it no longer appeals. The change is within us – a thankfulness for the miracles which are taking place daily; the blessings of health, family and friends. I am aware that these things can be taken from us in a moment of time. A man I once knew had the most marvellous voice – his talents were numerous. Yet without warning a massive stroke robbed him of speech, rendering him unable to use his limbs and totally reliant on others. He is now unable to communicate, just like our daughter once was.

One day at a time

So I ask you, God, to help me live one day at a time for your word tells me tomorrow will take care of itself. Keep me from being aware of just myself and family. Don't let me run from the needs of the lonely and suffering men and women. Don't let me be indifferent to the elderly and their fears. Prompt me to care, for I know what I do for them is as if it was done for you.

Life is very short and very demanding. The clock governs our lives. We glance at it most of the day. But do we use those precious hours wisely or are we preoccupied with things that are not important? I have discovered that when times in my life have been hec-

My Diane

tic and stressful it has been my own fault, because I couldn't say "No" to family or friends. Yet God often has to take "No" as an answer when we put off doing his will and abort his plans for our lives.

At this moment in time I can say I am contented with my life, with my God and the knowledge that he is the only one who will never let me down. He is my forever friend. There are no limits to what he will do if we trust him and that's just what I've done through all of Diane's life. Today I am reaping the results through persistent prayer, with its close companions, faith and patience.

Chapter 12
The final curtain

A home without curtains is unthinkable – they are invaluable and have a variety of uses: the humble door curtain that keeps out the draught, the elegant drapes that make the lounge look complete and the bedroom curtains drawn backwards and forwards each day shutting us in from the dark night sky and then revealing another new day each morning. The curtains in the theatre, so rich looking and heavy, are used as a screen, rising up as the performance begins and coming down when the show is over.

Shakespeare likened the world to a stage with the men and women in it merely players. Most of us put on an act, wearing a variety of masks, afraid of people seeing us as we really are. Only within our own homes might we drop the pretence.

My Diane

I remember the day when a shy young woman was thrust out onto the world's stage. Her name was Diana Spencer. Every part of her life was revealed to an eager audience worldwide. As the curtain rose it revealed an imperfect, shyly glancing young woman who, by the end of the performance, would become a star and the idol of millions.

Momentum gathered as Diana made more of an impact each time she made a public appearance. In a short time the inexperienced Spencer girl became the Princess of Wales. Her popularity exceeded that of Prince Charles and the media were quick to realise the newsworthiness of this very photogencic and stylish young woman.

It would seem the nation loved her and were interested in every little word printed about her. Whether the mask was on or off didn't trouble her public. When 'warts and all' were revealed it made no difference but only served to draw the public even closer. Thus the "People's Princess" was born – someone who was not like the rest of us, yet had the common touch, with that added compassion which became her trademark. Yet, sadly, the people's princess who was portrayed as vibrant and full of life stepped into a car one fateful evening that would take her on a journey from which there would be no return. The whole nation was stunned, its grief portrayed in the millions of

The final curtain

flowers laid, and the silent vigil of the many who came to mourn outside Kensington Palace.

When my dear father passed away we sat at the crematorium watching the curtain slowly closing, knowing it was parting us from our loved one.

The last curtain that comes to mind is found recorded in the Bible. It was situated in the temple. Only the High Priest could enter the holy place. When Jesus cried out, "It is finished!" as he hung on the cross, the Bible says the curtain was torn in two from top to bottom, signifying that the way was now open between a Holy God and man. Christ had reconciled us to his Father. Because Jesus died and rose again he took the sting out of death for us, giving us the chance to receive abundant life now and eternal life to come. He brought healing in every way to us through his great sacrifice. "By his stripes we are healed."

Everything is reversed

Our daughter, Diane, was not living, just existing. Her life was the complete opposite to the late Princess's life, yet through being set free the curtain is going up for my Diane. Everything is reversed. She is loved by so many people now. Her looks have changed. She is so pretty. She has joined a fitness club and is learning to swim.

My Diane

Last week just thrilled my heart. Our friend, Rya Gorman had asked Diane to sing a solo at the Friendship Hour held at Pastor Cliff Henderson's church. I just bowed my head and prayed, "Father, I release Diane to you. Anoint her as she sings. Please show these people what you have done for her."

She got up from her seat, picked up the microphone and sang to the backing tape "More love, More Power, More of you in my life". She never made one mistake, she was just perfect. Pastor Cliff stood at the back of the church, his eyes full of tears knowing his prayers had not been in vain.

I know this is a new beginning for Diane. Life will only get better for her. The way forward is going to be bright and fulfilling. Talents and gifts are ready to be released now. You might ask "How can you know, Barbara?" I reply, "Because I believe God's word, calling those things that are not as if they were."

Many times when writing this book doubt kept coming into my mind. "You can't write a book, Barbara, you couldn't write a decent essay at school. This is way out of your depth; it will never be published."

God is so good. He confirmed to me that I was in his will being led by him. The editor of Joy Magazine rang me to say Diane's story would soon be published in the magazine. He wasn't sure which month. The

The final curtain

timing was right, we couldn't believe it. On the cover was Princess Diana and just inside was our Diane, which brings me right back to the beginning of this book.

The day I started the book the news had come on the television that Diana, Princess of Wales, aged 36, had been tragically killed. The final curtain had come down on the People's Princess.

At age 33, my Diane's life is just beginning after being healed and restored by another whose life was tragically cut short at the very same age. He died that we all might live. His name is Jesus, the son of the living God.

My Diane